Money Stacking

The Inevitable Way of Financial Growth

By: Steve Mason

9781635011500

I0510908

PUBLISHERS NOTES

Disclaimer – Speedy Publishing LLC

This publication is intended to provide helpful and informative material. It is not intended to diagnose, treat, cure, or prevent any health problem or condition, nor is intended to replace the advice of a physician. No action should be taken solely on the contents of this book. Always consult your physician or qualified health-care professional on any matters regarding your health and before adopting any suggestions in this book or drawing inferences from it.

The author and publisher specifically disclaim all responsibility for any liability, loss or risk, personal or otherwise, which is incurred as a consequence, directly or indirectly, from the use or application of any contents of this book.

Any and all product names referenced within this book are the trademarks of their respective owners. None of these owners have sponsored, authorized, endorsed, or approved this book.

Always read all information provided by the manufacturers' product labels before using their products. The author and publisher are not responsible for claims made by manufacturers.

This book was originally printed before 2014. This is an adapted reprint by Speedy Publishing LLC with newly updated content designed to help readers with much more accurate and timely information and data.

Speedy Publishing LLC

40 E Main Street, Newark, Delaware, 19711

Contact Us: 1-888-248-4521

Website: http://www.speedypublishing.co

REPRINTED Paperback Edition: ISBN: 9781635011500

Manufactured in the United States of America

DEDICATION

This book is dedicated to my lovely life. You are always with me in every ups and downs.

TABLE OF CONTENTS

Chapter 1- Family Frugal Living to Boost Financial Growth

Family budgeting is very different from the budget requirements of a couple. The needs of a family unit differ greatly from that of a couple without the commitments of having children. Get all the info you need here.

A good and fully comprehensive family finance planning exercise should ideally include items such as dreams, goals, resources and responsibilities of the entire family unit.

This is to ensure all possible bases are cover for the long term planning, thus creating a better overview of the future direction the family should take.

This is also a good way to design the path and work toward the goals set as a family unit. The positive element often enjoyed by this form of planning would include all parties working together and gaining good and practical experiences along the way.

Money Stacking

In a lot of cases, the planning of the family budget both in long term and short term formats help to bring the family closer and more capable of handling hiccups along the way.

Family finance planning basics should also ideally take on the element of creating a comfortable leeway for unwanted surprises that are almost certain to happen along the way as the family grows and evolves.

Learning how inspire the family to go along with the expenses prepared is also another important element that can be experienced with the planning exercise.

The entire family will learn to adapt the respective needs and indulgences according to the financial plan drawn. Having discussions and being clear on the financial situation of the family will help instill a sense of responsibility with each family member thus ensuring all work as one unit to make the financial commitment of the family manageable.

The other benefit of family financial planning is also to get the children involved at a very early age, in the various components, commitments and sacrifices the parents would be making on their behalf so that they are able to enjoy a better quality of life.

Evaluate Family's Finances

It would be a good idea to practice periodic financial evaluation for the better understanding of the family's financial standing. This is also important; as it will help the family make the necessary adjustments should there be a need for such changes.

The net worth of a family is always changing and this is mostly due to outside factors that are beyond the control of the family unit.

Therefore periodic evaluation exercises will help the parents better adjust to these changes and make informed decisions of the future of the family's financial standing.

Sometimes this may include the need to make some cut backs on spending or it may also present some positive saving of which the family may decide to enjoy immediately, or even the prospect of reinvesting any access finances for further gain.

All these decisions can only be done when the whole family is committed to positively contributing to the general finances of the family.

When the help of the whole family is enlisted, any small progress or saving can have quite a liberating effect on the family unit as a whole, as it will help to show the positive results of a family working together for the better good of all.

The motivation that can be gotten out of the family unit being able to manage their finances will is also another positive outcome from this type of family cooperation.

Through the evaluation process of the current financial standing of the individual and the family unit as a whole, other decisions on Investment can be made.

If the financial situation allows for a bigger investment portfolio without adversely affecting the current spending power of the family, then such opportunities should be capitalized upon.

However as in all commitments, some caution should be exercised, so as not to over extend one's self.

Set a Family Financial Goal

Getting the family involved at some level of the family financial planning and goal settings will be beneficial to all parties, especially the kids, as they will be able to see firsthand just what it entails to run a family successfully and comfortably.

The perseverance and commitment needed to create a suitable and workable family financial plan will also create a new appreciation by the children for the parents for their willingness to share the fruits of their labor with their children.

Ideally this should be achieved through the arranging of a family meeting to work out the details of the financial goals for the family unit. The following should be some of the elements included in the process of the family meeting for finance planning:

A meeting should be called to discuss the aspirations and goals the family should be working towards as a unit. There should be some level of encouragement for all participating members of the family to be able to express their own individual opinions without reservations.

The key to raising children who are conscious and careful about spending habit is to inculcate very early on in life the merits of budgeting and sticking to the budget designed.

Items such as college funds, car upgrades, large house expenses, retirement funds should all be discussed and clearly outlined for all the members to be encouraged to understand the general commitments of the family income.

Getting all the relevant document such as financial records and then taking the time to evaluate the financial situation honestly will help greatly in the eventual financial planning stage.

Getting all the family members to be willing to eliminate any unnecessary expenses and frivolous spending is also another positive attitude to encourage through the family meeting.

Unnecessary Spending

Sometimes after and evaluation has been done on the family's financial situation, it is found that some changes needs to be made in order for the family to function comfortable without getting into debts. This would require an in depth study of the current spending habits of the family and also reviewing where changes can be made.

The following are some suggestions on how to go about successfully eliminating extra spending without causing undue inconvenience and stress:

Perhaps the first step to initiate would be to compile a list on exactly how the income is being spent.

By determining where the money is being spent, the individual or the family unit will be able to work as a team to identify areas where cut backs are possible and workable.

Once these areas have been identified, the next step would be to actually start making the changes as soon as possible so that immediate overall financial commitments can be decreased.

This would include unnecessary purchases and indulgences that are no longer totally necessary and considered frivolous. The most effective and quick way to being spending under control would be to go shopping with a list compiled of needs rather than wants, and to diligently stick to the list no matter what bargains are available for items not on the list.

Cutting down on entertainment, especially when it is done in an expensive manner is another way to eliminate extra spending. Instead of going out on the town, arrange to have home parties where everyone chips in for food and drinks.

This will not only be an adventurous way of entertaining but would probably be better than some noisy nightclub or expensive restaurant where the bill does not really justify the food ordered.

CHAPTER 2- FAMILY BUDGET, FINANCES IN ORDER

The most obvious result of not being financially savvy would be the chances on incurring huge debts would be very high indeed. However it should be noted that with a little thought and help, it is possible to keep one's finances in order, so as not to be burdened in the future with mounting problems.

There are a lot of dangers that the individual or family unit will encounter along the way if there is no control or format laid out for financial order.

One of the dangers would be to fall so far into debt, that it would be very difficult and sometimes impossible to get out from under these acuminated debts.

Money Stacking

In some cases there is simply no recourse that can be taken other then resorting to declaring one's self a bankrupt. This is the worst possible scenario to be in, therefore before matters reach anywhere near this level, step should be taken to minimize spending.

When finances are not in order, is would be impossible to spend wisely as there would not really be any clear list on what and where the priority for spending should be.

The danger would be to simply and blindly spend on everything and anything without keeping proper records or tracking the spending habits, thus causing a lot of damage to the financial credibility of the individual. This of course will eventually affect the family and their needs too.

You and Your Partner

Being able to achieve some level of being financially in sync as a couple is very beneficial to any relationship. Couples already have to face a lot of challenges without having the extra burden of having to contend with family finances.

The following are some suggestions on how to go about finding some common ground for the purpose of ensuring financial possibilities of getting everything in sync:

Perhaps the first step or exercise to attempt would be to disclose any and all financial records. This is the best way to start as both parties will be able to work out honestly where and how the money is coming in and going out.

Understanding this process will also allow the couple to make all the necessary adjustment to ensure there are no future financial disputes within the relationship.

It is very important to be forth coming and very honest at this stage about each other financial credentials.

Once this is clearly mapped out, the next step of discussion and initiating financial goals can be tackled. Discussing future financial goals will also create a stronger bond of cooperation if both parties are agreeable to the goals set.

Working towards these goals can be a very pleasant experience especially if both parties are equally committed.

Once the goals are set, the couple can move on to making their own financial budgeting agenda.

Here too the couple would need to work together to help each other have a better hold on their commitments and spending power. It is usually easier to budget when there is a check and balance format in place to guide the individual along.

Respecting each other's needs for certain indulgences is also another important element to be conscious off when trying to stay in sync with each other financially. Therefore it would be a good idea not to be to controlling in this area.

Having Fun for Less

Although some people may scoff at the idea of "cheap fun", this is often the most enjoyable time people will attest to experiencing. The idea is to be able to have fun without the whole episode costly

Money Stacking

such a huge amount of money that the possibility of chalking up debts is very real indeed.

The following are some great ways to have fun without breaking the bank:

It is not always necessary to stay home to have cheap fun. There are places the family unit can go together without actually having to incur a lot of costs.

One of the most popular ways would be to go on a picnic. Packing food from home would be the first step in saving cost and licking a location that is both safe and conducive yet near enough not to incur transportation costs would be another plus.

Going on a nature hike is also another cheap way to have fun. Here the family unit will be able to enjoy the exercise together and at the same time learn to appreciate the outdoors and all its many fascinating elements it has to offer for free.

If the family unit is very fond of reading, a trip to the library where hours of reading fun can be experienced for free is another option to enjoy.

This would be cost effective as purchasing material to read can be rather expensive and not really worth the cost it can chalk up in the long run. For those who are culturally inclined, going to the museum and various cultural exhibits would also be comparatively cost effective.

Other activities such as kite flying, going to the beach, walking in the park, playing outdoor games can all be good and cheap, yet great family building activities to indulge in.

When finances are not in order, there is also the possibility of losing the current lifestyle enjoyed, simply because those responsible for payments can no longer make them. This pressure will not only cause the individual to be frustrated but will also contribute to severely damaging any relationships and family units.

Chapter 3- Financial Assistance: Wise Move or Not?

Everyone today views a good educational background as a tool that is both important and instrumental in ensuring a comfortable and good quality of adult life. However for some this may be something that is out of reach simply due to the sometimes exorbitant fees linked to the educational program desired.

In view of this, several institutions have designed educational financial help, to be extended to those in need or to those who qualify for such assistance. Most of these financial aids are given out based on an individual merits. The pay back payments for such schemes is usually only expected when the said individual is gainfully employed, which is normally upon completion of the course.

However for those lucky few, whose parents had taken out educational policies or who had started putting towards an educational fund for their children this particular assistance is usually not necessary.

These policies are usually started when the child in question, is still at a very young age, thus providing the less pressured option to the parents who may otherwise have to come up with huge amounts of money for payments toward the child's education.

The governing bodies of the time also do their bit to help those with educational commitments by providing incentives like tax cuts.

These tax cuts or rebates of sorts will also help to lessen the burden on the young working adult who has to pay off educational loans besides all the other daily living expenses.

There are also other alternative such as scholarships which are periodically offered to anyone who fulfils the criteria imposed by the institution extending the scholarships.

Some of these do not require any payback but instead "ties" the individual to the company for an agreed amount of time. For some this is looked upon as an advantage as the individual is assured of a job upon completion of the course taken.

Financial Independence

Education is something that should be enjoyed by all, however in a lot of cases it may not be possible for women to enjoy the same privileges extended to men.

Some of the reasons this is prevalent is due to cultural backgrounds, need to provide an income for the family from a very young age, suppression from elders and finances. Of all the reasons finances is one that can possibly be overcome with a little outside help.

Money Stacking

The following are some tips on how to acquire some level of financial independence to ensure one is able to commit to an educational program:

Getting a part time job to supplement the fees for the education program chosen is one way of starting out the road to financial independence.

A lot of people today particularly women work at day jobs or part time jobs to pay for their educational needs. Though somewhat exhausting at times it can also be a good motivating factor that keep the individual focused on doing well and finishing the course as quickly as possible as the education received would then contribute to the possibility of securing a better job.

Some fields require the workforce to ideally be women thus the relevant institutions are more than willing to extend financial help to any woman seeking such assistance.

There are also a few agencies that specifically cater to the financial needs of women, as they recognize the need and the importance the women can play in the work force.

Study loans are also another form of financing that the woman can apply for in the quest to have access to funds to pay for the intended course or program. Such funds are usually given out based on the merits of an individual.

How to Get Financial Aid

Financial aid is something that most people would like to enjoy when it comes to paying for education. As education is becoming increasingly expensive and out of reach for some there is a need to look for ways to acquire such funds for the pursuit of higher education.

The following are some tips on how to get this desired financial aid:

Scholarships and fellowships – most of these are given out based on the merits of an individual though the categories of assessments may vary.

These many include the need to have any one of the following features; athletic ability, academic merit, disability and any other criteria at the time.

Grants – this is a form of assistance that is usually given out to those below a certain family income level. In most cases there is no necessity to pay off such amount extended to the student, as the financial capability of the family is taken into consideration.

Academic competitive grants – this is also another form of assistance that does not require any payback stipulations but is given out based on competency and the competitiveness of all the participant vying for the grant.

Some of the qualifying requirements may be that the students would have to make presentations or inventions that would convince the governing body to award the grant to the winning individual.

There are also institutional grants whereby individual attending such institutions are awarded the grants based on individual merit and needs.

For those intending to attend such facilities there is a possibility of applying for this type of assistance. When given the amount is usually enough to cover the cost of the education only. All other expenses incurred would have to be borne by the individual.

Although the fees can be a help there is still the burden of having to pay for living expenses and others.

Financing Your Education

Planning for anything is always a good idea, and planning for education is no exception. There is a real need to look into the area of planning for future needs for financial education as it is mostly no longer free and can actually be quite costly. Thus planning and starting some kind of fund geared towards educational needs would certainly be a wise and very much needed exercise.

There are several types of educational policies that can be taken out by parents or guardians on behalf of their children and this can be one of the easiest ways of eventually paying for costly educational needs.

Such plans or policies can be taken out when the child in question is still at a very young age, thus by the time the funds are actually physically needed the initial sum would have amounted to quite a good amount.

This can then be put towards paying off part, if not all of the fees for the educational program chosen. This style not only eliminates the stressful situation that is usually brought on by the need to source for financing, it can also help to discipline the individual into making a long term commitment towards the future.

There are also other resources that can be tapped into, if the individual is savvy enough to understand and find such existing resources.

These may include financial aid that consist of loans, grants, scholarships and work study programs. Some of these are awarded based on the merits of the applicant while others can be given out based on the needs of the applicant.

Most government organizations focus on the sector that applies for such aid based on need.

Looking for tax breaks can also be one reason to start an educational policy or fund for children. There are various tax benefits extended to those making a conscious effort to put aside money for the purpose of education.

CHAPTER 4- ECONOMIC STATUES AND YOUR EDUCATION FINANCING

Every movement of the economy whether it for the better or worse, will eventually affect all those depending on the various aids extended by both governing bodies and institutions. As such some measures should be taken to ensure the impacts are not felt so severely that the education sector is left in a poor state.

Whenever there are financial problems or challenges, one of the sectors that usually feel the brunt of such disruptions is the educational sector.

Therefore there is a need to focus on trying to avoid such a possible scenario where funds to aid those intending to further their education are limited or nonexistent.

Starting an educational fund very early on and making contributions in a disciplined way will help when outside assistance is harder to come by. Allocations for such funds can be done on a periodical deduction or deposit style.

Taking out an education policy is also something that is quite a common practice for most young parents as they would like to be in a position where they can adequately provide for their children's education.

However when an economic downturn begin to effect the earning power of the said parent there should be some clause in the educational policy that caters to such possibilities.

Picking an educational policy that has these added benefits is very useful as the parent should ensure nothing effects the premium payments to keep the policy on going.

Sometimes the demographics statistics of the time can also affect the availability of the aid for educational purposes.

There may be an influx of a particular choice in a particular field where there is simply not enough funds or seats for the intended course.

Here measures are usually taken to narrow down the interested parties to those who would be most eligible for taking up the course and the financial aid given.

Planning Education Expenditure

Being able to provide a comfortable amount that will eventually cover all expenses during the course of the study plan is an essential element to consider when planning and budgeting for education. It would be quite disruptive for the student, should the fund be found to be inadequate, thus dictating that certain part of the studying experiences would not be coved thus causing anxiety which will eventually affect the quality of the studying process.

Money Stacking

The following are some areas within the educational expenditure that should be given due consideration to ensure adequate funds are set aside to cater to all aspects listed:

It is quite common to only take into account the actual fees the course might require to be paid. Taking into account all the relevant assisting tools that may be required for the course is only sometimes considered unless the course specifically states it importance or the course revolves around the use of such tools. Therefore taking into account just the actual fees only is not enough.

There should also be funds set aside for any miscellaneous items that may be required for use during the course. As some of these items can be quite costly there is a need to have a good amount of funds available to this. Failing to provide for such expenses can also affect the quality of the learning experience.

If the course requires some form of insurance coverage this should also be taken into consideration as part of the expenditure that could be deemed necessary to incur.

The cost of some insurance policies can be a fairly large amount and there may be no allowances given to make such payments in staggered form.

Calculating the rise in inflation and the devaluation of the currency is also another important element to consider as what may be deemed suitable now, may not even cover the initial fees amount in the future.

Tax and Education Financing

In the quest to encourage as many people as possible to reach out for better educational assistance there are various step the governing bodies of the time have initiated for such assistance. This assistance may also take the form of tax breaks for those individual paying for their own educational needs.

The following are some area where and how such tax reliefs can be enjoyed:

Tax claims can be made on most expenses pertaining to the use for educational tools for the study programs enrolled in or for the actual fees that are required to be paid.

These claims can be made on an individual basis or on behalf of the child requiring such funds. Independent student educational programs are usually also included as eligible for tax breaks.

In some areas the items specifies in the legislation as an eligible educational tool, expense or requirement can also be used to make claims for tax relief.

Such claims can be put forward upon immediate commencement of the course in question. Such tools may include home computers and laptops, computer related equipment, internet connection services, course materials, books and learning aids and many other corresponding elements that would be essential to the learning process within the course frame.

Some saving accounts also offer tax relief on the interests earned if the funds are to be used for educational purposes. Therefore saving in such accounts will definitely be a profitable and good option to start.

Money Stacking

There are many different programs offered by both government agencies and private institutions alike and all with the added incentive of receiving tax breaks. All this is designed to encourage and make education more accessible to the massed on the higher education scale.

Employer paid education is also another area where tax reliefs are given. Here both the employer and employee benefit from encouraging and participating in educational programs.

Become educated on all the different ways to fund your education and you will be able to go thru school without the added financial worries.

CHAPTER 5- WHEN BUSINESS TALKS, MONEY TALKS

In simple terms, venture capitalists are usually comprised of a group of investors with a lot of funds, ready to invest in any business venture that might present good possibilities of success.

This form of investment can come in the form of one very wealthy individual or from a group of wealthy individuals, intent on investing into a venture that has promising prospects.

There are also companies designed and set up for the purpose of sourcing for and investing in startup businesses and already small successful businesses that may be looking to expand their operation, but lack the financial backing needed. The venture capitalist play a very important role in extending such financial help to those looking for financial backing but don't have the proper credential to approach establishments such as banks, government loan institutions or finance houses.

Besides being noted for their financial capabilities, the venture capitalists can also provide other skills such as managerial and technical expertise. These too may provide invaluable assistance to those lacking in this area but still possess a winning formula for making phenomenal money.

Most venture capitalist financing sources come from a pool of wealthy investors, investments banks and other financial institutions that pool their mainly monetary resources to form investments arms that popularly extend financial assistance to promising business ventures. However because of the nature the extension, there is also what may seem like a disadvantage tagged to such assistance and this would come in the form of the said investors wanting to play an active in the business entity. For most business ventures seeking financial assistance, this form of "interference" would present an ideal situation or solution.

Thus, in addition to actually having some equity in the company, the venture capitalist expects to be involved in some level or another to ensure the investments are going in the direction intended.

How to be a Venture Capitalist

It is quite normal, in fact very necessary to ask questions before investing into anything, especially when it involves a considerable amount of capital. Venture capital investments, usually entail a substantial amount being lent towards a business endeavor, without the backing of any tangible assets, therefore the questioning exercise is only to be expected.

The following are some of the questions that should be asked before venturing into the capital investment game:

• Perhaps the foremost question to be asked is about the actual business and what it is all about. Facts should be established as to what the business intends to accomplish and within what time frame. As for the individual seeking the funds, there should be a sales pitch that coves all these issues and presented in a confident and powerful manner to grab the attention of the potential capital investor.

• Questioning the level of competitive presence and how the business entity is prepared to tackle this issue should also be done. Ensuring the business owner is aware of the competition and the tactics used by the competitors is something that needs to be explored. This is to ensure there are no unpleasant surprises sometime into the investment program. It would also give the capital investor an idea of just how wholesome the business strategy is for the company that is seeking the funds.

• Through the consideration process, the capital investor should also ensure the business entity intended for the investment is already prepared with a supporting and strong customer base. This is an essential aspect to question, as it will give the investor a projected view of the profits expected.

Internet Startup

It is an established fact that venture capitalists played a significantly important role in the financing of many internet startup companies. Without the assistance of these financing arms, the internet boom may not have had the opportunity to make any form of real impact at the time.

Unfortunately it was also a sobering experience due to the negative returns and declining investment levels which was quite the opposite of what was first being expected or projected. The changes brought on by the internet boom were phenomenal and perhaps the excitement caused or added to everyone jumping on the band wagon with the intention of grabbing some of the seeing easy profits, only to find there was very little to be had. However there are some that would disagree with this perceived outcome and the longs term outlook did show the more competent and better players within the internet bubble we able to hold their own. Statistically it was hard to come up with accurate fugues at the time as there were a lot of cases of under declaring losses.

At the time a lot of the internet companies had the innovative ideas but lack the proper management tools and finances to launch their businesses, thus the emergence of the capital venture's role in the equation.

Being able to provide the direction, the capital venture boom came about strongly, as it was able to have added value services to help professionalize the entities they chose to finance and to help establish both entities as formidable in the market. Successful companies could grow even faster and those experiencing losses still had the funds to make efforts to improve even if it seemed futile at the time. Venture capitalists platforms are already risky to start with, thus for some there may have been an overreaction to the upside and downside of the boom.

Chapter 6- Growing Your Business, Growing Your Money

Every business foray is started with the main intention of making money. Some business styles require hand on labor while some provide simply the expertise to the business equation. As for the venture capitalist, most of the time the contribution or participation comes in the form of finances.

The following are some of the ways the venture capitalists can make good money:

• Having the funds to invest is certainly an advantage, and this can prove to be even better when the individual is not savvy enough or disciplined enough, to actually venture into the business arena, to bring the business idea to reality. Therefore the next best option would be to use the funds available to invest in a business entity, which is similar to that of the one the investor would have been interested in starting up personally. In this way the investor would be part of a business entity where personal business "dreams" can be realized without the actual need for participation.

• Money can also be made when the capital investor is able to gain controlling shares with the business entity looking for funds. Not only does this assure the capital investor bigger profit percentages, but it also gives the capital investor the controlling power to dictate the direction the business is to take. If the business idea has phenomenal profit making possibilities, then the risks involved could be measurably lower thus making the exercise of capital investment worth the effort and time. The fast returns would also allow the capital investor to move on to other business opportunities.

• With wise investments made, there is also the probability of heightened visibility for the capital investment entity. This will create the ideal presence for the capitol investor, where prospective businesses will seek out the participation of such strong assisting partnerships.

Provide For Others

The most obvious assistance would be in creating the finances that helps to form companies that can then exists through the creating of jobs. However this is not the one and only role that the venture capitalist can play is creating jobs.

With the financial backing, new businesses are set up and these businesses will open the door to employment opportunities for the masses. No matter what industry the venture capitalist venture into the underlying fact remains the same, which is they provide the means and work possibilities for others. This is especially beneficial for a young economy looking for outside investors other than that provided for by the government. With the participation of such capital investors, new businesses can spring up thus contributing to the vibrancy of the young economy. The jobs created by the establishment of such businesses will help to contribute positively to the all parties involved from the investing arm to the end user which is the customer. The opportunities apparent for all levels are not only phenomenal but also immensely beneficial.

If the governing body at the time in interested in establishing a niche market for the country then venture capitalist would be their first choice of fund seeking assistance. With the assistance of such entities the job and expertise can be made available to the masses, and in doing so effectively provide the platform for churning out competency within the niche identified.

Venture capitalists are also considered an ideal source on expertise besides the more obvious financial investment it can provide. This is due to the fact that most capital investors are well versed in the fields of investment chosen, thus bringing along with them the very important training tools that would help to not only create jobs but also create competency within the business entity itself. The expertise brought to the equation, through the venture capitalists participation can include managerial tactical skills, initiatives on growth plans, identifying and solving potential problems and many other positive contributing factors.

The Perils

The general style in which the venture capitalist base the investments on, is in itself already cause for concern, as predominantly there is no recourse for collection on failed investments, should the entity invested in not perform as expected or according to par.

Money Stacking

Although extensive studies are usually conducted before deciding to invest in a particular business entity, there is no collateral asked for or given, to provide for any assurance toward the capital invested. This sort of risk is seemingly quite silly but for most investors such risks is heavily weighted against the prospects of considerable profits and controlling participation in the invested business.

Another risk in this type of investment arm is that there is no stability to count on, thus effectively depending entirely on the integrity of those involved to create the intended positive profits churning results. On paper, all the necessary points of the business entity may present very little or no problems at all, however when actual operations are up and running, this seemingly problem free business engine can start to cause unforeseen problems. This then will eventually eat into the finances originally set aside for the business entity, which may then lead to even further unforeseen setbacks. All this will add to the already preexisting risk factors that capital investors are used to.

If the capital venture group is not really savvy in the area chosen then there is also a possibility of making a less than desirable choice in when it comes to identifying viable business prospects.

Without the very valuable business background in a particular field taking calculated risks to invest without prior knowledge of the workings that would involve such a choice would be rather disastrous indeed. Being ill advised can also add to the heightened risk ratio for the capital investor.

Let's face it; investing can be scary, especially when investing in businesses blindly with no backing. Investing is a great way to sit back and rack in the profits. Before beginning you should take the time to retain the information and tips that were in this book. If

Steve Mason

you follow this steps and guidelines you are sure to succeed and make a good living in the process.

CHAPTER 7- YOUR 100 TIPS TO MAKE MORE MONEY

Have you grown tired and fed up slaving for ten to twelve hours every single day, earning just a little over the minimum wage?

Like many, you may feel like your desk has become more of a prison cell that has kept you all locked away from the rest of civilization. And still, you find yourself living from paycheck to paycheck.

Time, they say, is money.

If that's the case, this brings home the fact that some people are certainly making a whole lot more money in the same amount of time you are willing to put in, or even at a considerably far lesser time.

By now, you have probably deduced the fact that there has got to be a better way to play the money---making game.

Yes. In fact, there are a hundred different better ways to play the game.

It is possible to earn more by working less. You've seen other people do it. It's time to write your own success story and make it happen in your life.

While increasing your productivity will give you twice as much return, discovering a far better way to play the game will possibly bring you twenty times or more return.

According to Robert Collier, "Success they say is the sum of small efforts, repeated day in and day out."

Every single time you find a better way of doing something ------ whether it's a faster route to earning that salary raise or a more efficient approach to going through your daily emails ------ you unlock a powerful solution to earning more simply because your time has become more valuable and now worth more money.

But the question is how do you exactly do that? How do you get to the point where you spend lesser amount of time working and yet earning better?

The "secrets" to earning more are actually all around you. You probably have next door neighbors who are raking in a fortune doing things you never have even thought of.

Time is money.

It's about time you figure out how highly successful people spend their valuable time.

Money Stacking

1 Learn the money--making potential of affiliate programs. This is one popular and very effective way to earn passive income, which is derived from setting up a website that pre---sells company products. In this setup, the company provides the products along with the programming code that tracks down sales, of which you will be given a commission for every successful sale. Find companies that are known to offer bigger commissions as well as track down clients who are highly likely to make multiple purchases over extended period of time, which will generate recurring commissions.

2 Create information products such as eBooks.

The web provides a great way to create and sell an eBook that explains "How To" information, such as How to Start Your Online Business, or any other topic designed to provide information on how to make life easier for people. There is a huge demand of information, which is something you can capitalize on. The great thing with eBook is it's easier to create, which you can complete at a short amount time. Once done, you simply have to come up with a website, secure a web hosting service and set up your own online marketing in place. This will make it possible for your eBooks available for purchase 24 hours a day, for several years to come, with the possibility of earning income while you sleep.

3 Earn passive residual income through advertising commissions.

If you own a website or you are planning to own one, work on attracting visitors or generating web traffic by providing relevant, original and fresh content to attract people to visit your sites. By allowing banner placements or links on your site at a certain fee, you can look forward to collecting passive residual income every month.

4 Become a reseller of web hosting services or domain registration.

Offer web hosting service wherein you simply pay a monthly fee and resell the service at a certain subscription charge to your customers. However, if you are planning to engage in this type of service, it is important to be thoroughly familiar and knowledgeable with the web hosting service in order to provide prompt and reliable support to your customers.

5 Master the art of salary negotiation.

During job interviews, instead of waiting for the salary conversation to be tackled, you can go right ahead and ask the interviewer/recruiter the expected salary of the position you are applying for. This way you don't have to waste time going back and forth with negotiations since you already know the figures and can decide ahead of time if it's something viable enough for you to pursue your application.

6 Keep your emails short and concise.

Instead of spending precious minutes composing long and winding emails, keep everything short and to the point. Firstly, your subject line should be informative so your recipients will know if it is something they need to prioritize. When conveying your message in a direct manner, make sure to avoid constructing sentences in passive voice.

7 Get business and sales leads efficiently by directly asking people if they have a problem you can help resolve.

For example, if you are offering web design services, instead of checking out if there are people interested in having a new website, ask direct questions, such as "Who among you isn't happy

Money Stacking

with their current website?" This effectively cuts down the chase and you get to save significant amount of time when it comes to getting responses.

8 When it comes to working with a team, most of the time 80% accurate is good enough.

As you know, time is money and most of the time large projects have time--- constraints. If you are working with a team, achieving 80% accuracy is almost always good enough. You can leave the remaining 20% for the practicing or testing phase, where you can work out the finer details. Keep in mind that getting the job done right and on time is more important that getting all the details right.

9 Talk to a human customer service representative.

When calling customer service, instead of talking to an automated machine, get faster and more efficient resolution and support by going straight to a real person. If you have an important or urgent complaint, try to check contacthelp.com or gethuman.com if there is a code for the specific company you need to call and bypass the automated systems.

10 Master the art of saying "No."

Before making any commitments, evaluate your current workload and respect your limits. Learning to say no will not only free up your time but will also save you from a lot of stress. Successful people know what they want and have no trouble being decisive, putting their foot down on something and saying no.

11 Learn the art of delegation.

If you are the type of person used to doing everything on your own or you have difficulty of letting go, keep in mind that you do not have enough hours in the day to do and attend to everything. This is a very important value every managers and leaders should learn and accept. Reduce your workload and enhance efficiency by learning to delegate tasks.

12 Study to get training for a specialized skill.

These days, a highly desirable and specialized skill set can propel you from being just an ordinary employee to a more valuable one. Take time to determine what are the most valuable and in demand skills in your industry and check if it is something that you can learn to acquire during your spare time.

13 Earn a higher qualification or degree.

There are certain job sectors that require having a certain degree, specialized training or certificate in order to qualify you to a higher pay scale. While this route may be financially challenging and time consuming, it can increase your qualifications and make you eligible for promotions or higher designations, which can prove to be a good and rewarding investment in the long run. Whether it's an MBA degree or a Six Sigma Black Belt, check out if spending on night classes and seminars can turn out to be feasible investments. There are also companies that sponsor further education for qualified employees, so take time to discuss this with your company's Human Resource Department.

14 Consider changing your work hours or telecommuting.

If your employer is unable or unwilling to give you a salary raise in compensation of the amount of work you do, try to negotiate adjusting your work hours or discuss telecommuting options.

However, this may not work for a number of industries but if you can complete most of your work from home, then it's definitely worth asking. You can also evaluate your work hours and check if working on another shift can help your productivity or open up more time to pursue other money---making opportunities.

15 Instead of working as a full--timer, consider becoming a consultant.

If you are constantly working above and beyond the regular 40---hour work week, you may want to explore the idea of working as an hourly consultant, if it is more feasible financially. While this may not mean you work any less, this offers you more flexible work hours, thereby allowing you to take on additional clients and earn extra income instead of working full---time and not getting overtime pay.

16 Demand a salary raise if you are doing more or contributing significantly.

If you feel you deserve a raise for the amount of profit you are bringing in to your company or you are doing more work than you are originally hired to do, by all means ask for a raise based on your performance. You can time your request for a raise after a performance review. If you prove to be a great asset to the company, the management won't mind paying you more to retain your services.

17 Find an efficient way of doing repetitive tasks.

If your work or day to day tasks require you to attend to repetitive tasks on regular basis, instead of spending a significant amount of time completing them, try to figure out how you can automate or streamline the entire process. There are a lot of online applications and software products online designed to cut down the nitty---gritty stuff. Make use of free apps, which can significantly cut down the amount of time to complete a certain task. If you feel it's time to purchase paid software, bring this up with the management and make sure to come armed with reasons to justify the expense. Overall, these software can help in significantly increasing productivity, accuracy and provide easy access to organized information.

18 Consider changing jobs or making a bold career move.

If you feel your career is facing a dead end and there is no opportunity to transition into a more rewarding and healthier work---life balance with your current job, consider exploring better opportunities. Find a new work environment where your experience and skills are greatly valued. The bottom line here is, if you are overworked and underpaid, it's time you do something about it.

19 Consider taking on freelance writing jobs.

If you have a flair for writing or possess a solid grasp of good grammar, communication and spelling, you may want to seek opportunities for freelance writing jobs. You can contribute articles to magazines, newspapers and other local periodicals to earn extra income. Gradually build your portfolio and work your way towards establishing credibility.

20 Teach a language.

Do you know and speak another language? Or maybe you have strong command of the English language to qualify you to teach it? This is an in demand skill that can open up great money making opportunities.

21 Perform Internet research jobs.

If you are confident that you know your way around the web, you can offer your skill as an online researcher to local businesses.

22 Become a "green" consultant.

People are keen on making lifestyle changes that can result to using less energy for their home. This is a huge industry that can help you rake in significant profit by evaluating homes and making recommendations on how to become "green". Over time, you can also sell your services to companies.

23 Sell organic produce.

If you love gardening and know organic methods, consider selling organic produce. Depending on just how large your harvest is, you can offer "in season" organic vegetables as well as fresh herbs to restaurants. Chefs are always keeping an eye on suppliers that offer the best and the freshest.

24 Sell antiques and vintage pieces on eBay.

If you have good knowledge on antiques, spend your weekends scouting among thrift stores and garage sales as well as flea markets where you can potentially score old, valuable treasures on the cheap. Conduct a bit of a research and auction it off on eBay.

25 Get paid to shop.

There are a number of companies that actually hire people to perform what is known as "mystery shopping" and report their experiences to companies. When engaging in this type of job, you need to make sure to be fair and you possess a good grasp and understanding of the industry.

26 Decorate cakes.

If you love to bake, earn money on the side making and decorating cakes. Show off your baking prowess and offer to bake pastries as well as other goodies to local office break rooms, small coffee shops, local deli, etc.

27 Make and sell jams and jellies.

If you know how to can and preserve jams and jellies the old fashion way, you can make a large batch and sell jams and jellies that are in season. You can either choose to sell it among friends and colleagues, to a local market or even over the Internet.

28 Make money out of your photos.

If you own a fancy camera and you have a flair for taking stunning photos, put it to good use by offering your services to special events such as weddings, parties and corporate functions. You can also post them to online sites and make money every time someone decides to download and use it.

29 Take time to sort out your savings.

To earn more money, you need to make sure all you savings are working hard to earn profit. If you have a lump sum of money that you are prepared to put away for about 12 months or longer then get a fixed---rate account.

Money Stacking
30 Take in a lodger.

While most people spend a fortune to own a home, how about making your home earn and generate its own profit? If you have a spare room, consider renting it out and earn extra income on the side.

31 Rent out a car parking space.

If you are living close to the city center, or near a football stadium or train station, and you have a garage or parking space that you don't exactly use, it's a proverbial goldmine right under your nose. Rent your parking space to commuters or concert/game event fan and earn extra money on the side.

32 Sell on eBay.

You know what they say about one man's rubbish can turn out to be another man's treasure. If you have too many unused possessions that are taking up permanent residency in your basement and cramping your home, then consider auctioning pieces on eBay and earn money.

33 Answer paid surveys.

There are a number of online surveys available where you will be rewarded for your opinions, either through reward vouchers or cash.

34 Offer virtual assistance services.

With a growing number of web---based businesses today, virtual assistance services are now on very high demand. A lot of companies and people use the services of a virtual assistance to conduct researches, perform time---consuming jobs, find things and make phone calls, etc.

35 Make money by hosting an online forum.

Software such as SebFlipper has the ability to host a number of separate forums under a single server. You can make money by charging forum operators or owners for your hosting service. You can also offer this service for free and post your ads and banners on their forums to generate income.

36 Do podcasting.

This is similar to video or voice blogging where you can talk about some interesting topics and make money from the ads show. If you have a gift for gab, and you feel you can provide relevant information or interesting opinions, you can reach out to hundreds of subscribers through this platform.

37 Plan your day ahead and stick to it.

If you have try planning out your day and anticipate the possible roadblocks, you will find that you are better prepared to tackle challenges and deflect issues with more ease. This will help ensure you will have a more productive day.

38 Break down your large plans into more manageable milestones.

Try to achieve something worthwhile every day. If you plan out your goals and set schedules and timelines, you have more motivation not to slack off or procrastinate.

39 Start your day by tackling first the more difficult and the time--consuming tasks.

Money Stacking

This is the time where you still have full energy to go through everything before gradually moving on to easier ones.

40 Learn to best deal with interruptions in a decisive and assertive manner.

Do not allow the trivial concerns of others distract you from your purpose. This does not necessarily mean you need to be rude and offensive. Instead, learn to be firm and prioritize important things instead of constantly ending up accommodating other people's concerns.

41 Stop procrastinating.

Train yourself to avoid wasting time worrying or dawdling, which only increases your unproductivity. Remember, time is money. If you are constantly paralyzed with worry, schedule your 'worry time' at the end of each day so you can stay focused to tackle outstanding work and more important concerns.

42 Manage your clutter.

Make sure everything is in its proper place, this will save you time from constantly searching for misplaced items. A tidy desk can significantly help enhance productivity.

43 Stick to your priorities.

Don't get into the habit of cancelling or putting off things you can accomplish today. While one might say, you still have enough time tomorrow, it's another day to face with a whole new set of challenges.

44 Learn to batch process.

Bunch all the small and menial tasks that are not important. Instead of going to and fro attending to small things all throughout the day, which only interrupt and distract you from more important tasks, bundle or batch them together and go through them one set at a time. You can create a list of the small task and with only an hour or so left in your work day, start processing these tasks as quickly as possible, and crossing each one off your list.

45 Brown bag it.

While making and bringing your own lunch to work is not exactly life---changing, it saves you the unnecessary expense, free up more of your time by working through lunch and gives you better control of what you eat.

46 Take on high profile projects.

If you are constantly working on the sidelines, doing less important things, your accomplishments will certainly not make you a star, nor will it take you far. Instead, try to volunteer for bigger projects, the very ones that will carve your name and bring recognition to the company. If you have the expertise and confidence but there is a lack of worthwhile projects, consider coming up with your own. If you do well, these large and high---profile projects can make a huge impact on your career and life. These are the accomplishments that can enhance your portfolio.

47 Bank your salary raise.

If you were finally given a raise, don't immediately go into thinking of ways how to spend your extra money. Avoid increasing your expenditures. Instead, consider putting the entire amount in the bank.

48 Carefully organize your files and desk.

While they say creative minds can make sense of their own chaos, it can also add to stress and hamper your productivity. Label your folders accordingly and throw out papers and documents that can be discarded.

49 Tidy your to--do list.

If your to do list is about a mile long, go through each one and determine which ones are unnecessary. Develop the habit of eliminating unnecessary stuff and learn to simplify your life.

50 Get rid of distractions.

Eliminate all the unnecessary distractions such as IM and email alerts, Twitter and other social networking sites. In fact, if possible, you should consider turning off the Internet. You can also wear headphones so you will not be distracted with regular office noise.

51 Keep meetings to 30 minutes or less.

One of the most common and biggest time---wasters are meetings that could be easily accomplished with a phone call or an email. If possible, beg out of meetings, or if you call the shots, eliminate them if it's not critically important.

52 Only try to check your email once or twice a day.

Avoid constantly going through your emails all throughout the day. Allocate a time to go through your mail at the start of your day and check back an hour before you leave. If you keep on sending unimportant emails, you are creating major distractions to recipients and affecting the productivity of everyone, including yourself.

53 When at home, turn off your television.

One of the most effective ways to save you both time and money is to watch less television. This gives you more time to take care of more important things or seek a more rewarding hobby instead of watching all those guilt---inducing ads.

54 Go over your personal collection and check out which ones you can get rid and sell.

Turn a critical eye and determine if there are duplicates or items that you are willing to sell. While you are at it, how about considering cutting down the time you spend on your hobby and look for more profitable ventures? It would be great if you have a money---making hobby, or earn doing something you are passionate about. Who knows, this could open up a lot of great opportunities for you.

55 Practice the 30--day rule when contemplating on making a purchase.

If you are tempted to splurge or treat yourself with a latest gadget wait for 30 days and ask yourself if you really want the item. Often, the urge will pass away and you end up saving yourself a significant amount of money by waiting and not acting on impulse. It is important to train yourself to do away with the trivial and unnecessary purchases and save money on really sound investments.

Money Stacking

56 Avoid spending too much on entertaining your children. Instead of caving in to the temptation of buying your child the latest video game or the coolest gadget to hit the market, focus on honing his creativity and appreciate simple and stimulating games. It is important for parents to realize that children do not need fancy gadgets to keep them happy, instead make great memories spending more time with them, making stuff and discovering new things. You will definitely find these alternatives cheaper and more rewarding.

57 Contact your credit card company then ask for a rate reduction.

Choose any of your cards that are carrying a balance and call up the company number at the back part. Negotiate for an interest reduction or you will contemplate on taking your business elsewhere. If the person you talk to will not be able to accommodate your request, then ask for the supervisor. When you think about it, if you have $5, 000 worth of balance with a 3% reduction rate, you can potentially save $150 every year.

58 Clean out your closet.

Go through your wardrobe and focus on getting rid of some of the stuff. You can organize a yard sale or donate it to get a tax reduction. All the old stuff that are just sitting there can actually put more money into your pocket. Of course, it could also mean freeing up more closet space.

59 Choose term life insurance.

A lot of people believe that insurance is an investment. It is not. Switch to a term insurance instead then you can use the difference of the cost to settle some of your debts or start your savings. Whole and universal policies are significantly more expensive. You are definitely better off getting yourself out of debt instead of spending extra on sub---par investments.

60 When buying a car, go for fuel efficiency and reliability. Instead of going for what's popular or flashier, choosing a more fuel efficient and reliable car will save you thousands of dollars in the long run. For example, when driving a vehicle for 80, 000 miles, choosing a 25---mile per gallon car over a 15---mile per gallon will translate to 2, 133 gallons of gas. So if a gallon costs $3, that's an astonishing $ 6, 400 savings right there. In addition, reliability can also pay great dividends, so do your research. Your efforts will pay off for you, big time.

61 Avoid going to shopping centers and stores just for entertainment.

Indulging to the need to window shop will only encourage you to spend more money on stuff that you don't really need. Instead, seek other places to entertain you, such as the museum, the park or a friend's house. Don't substitute shopping as a form of entertainment and you will be better off.

62 Plan to invest on a small business and use business model that has a lot of potential of making you rich.

If you have not figured it out, entrepreneurs go into business since they have long realized working on a 9 to 5 job will not make them rich. However, going into business requires careful planning so make sure to cover all the bases. Start with a solid business model. If you can't see yourself raking in thousands or millions of dollars with your business idea, you may want to explore more possibilities.

63 Carefully identify and isolate your core strengths then decide to build on them.

Find something you truly enjoy, this is a strength that you can potentially build and invest on. If you go into a business, it is best to venture into something that will allow you to express your strengths then you can develop it more through repetition. A lot of people have successfully reaped great financial rewards following this route. Check out if you can cash in on yours.

64 Choose to operate in an industry with high demand and significant profit margin.

You make profit based on the difference on how much sales you make and the amount of money you keep from every sale after deducting the cost of delivering the goods or service. If you enjoy greater margin, then you will need a fewer amount of sales to earn a million. Before getting into any business, calculate first the possible margin of the products or service you choose to sell.

65 Opt to use cash.

Instead of constantly charging your purchases to your credit or debit cards, choose to pay in cash instead for all those non---bill spending such as gas, eating out and the groceries. Why? Paying in cash makes the experience of spending more real. There is also the fact that in choosing to spend cash, you have better control of your expenses instead of ending up spending more than you earn.

66 Make some minimal weekly savings transfers.

Try to deduct a few dollars off your disposable cash every week. You can start by transferring $20 or $40 per week and transfer it to your savings. It's a relatively small amount that you maybe barely notice but end up saving a large sum of money over a period of time.

67 Choose to stay home instead of going out.

Going out will encourage you to spend unnecessarily since you will be tempted to eat at restaurants, stop at the gas station, go to the mall, etc. It is difficult, almost impossible to avoid spending when you are on the road so stay at home instead and seek other free entertainment. You can also use this free time to spend with your family.

68 Avoid getting catalogs or any other emailed announcements.

All these emails and newsletters are all designed by companies to sell you stuff. When you frequently receive announcements of cool new products or upcoming sales, it can be very tempting to make a purchase on luxury items or service. Choose to stop all those catalog and newsletter subscriptions so you don't have to deal with trying to resist temptation.

69 Choose to cook at home instead of eating out.

This may be difficult to do especially if you are too tired to cook after a grueling day at work. Instead of expensive dinners or ordering deliveries and takeout fast food that are not exactly healthy, throw in a quick stir fry using fresh or frozen veggies. You can also research ahead of time some no---fuss and 10--- minute recipes, so cooking homemade and healthier dishes doesn't have to be a real burden.

70 Use the envelope system when segregating your money. This is following the same concept of paying cash. Use envelopes in order to split your disposable cash into the different categories. If you empty one envelope, then that means you have completely spent your allotment.

71 Learn the spreadsheet tracker hack.

There are a lot of expensive programs out there like Quicken, MS Money, etc. that can help you better manage your finances. However, you don't exactly need to invest in any of those fancy software, especially if you don't have a real need for all the bells and whistles that only cost you more. Instead, you can use Google Docs and Spreadsheets, which you can use to keep track of your bank account. You can indicate dates for every transaction, including titles and amounts, along with a little field for notes or memos and your running balance.

72 Choose to pay debt and savings first.

Every time you sit down to go through all your bills, choose to pay or allocate money first for your savings then make your debt payments. If you constantly choose to allocate money for your savings for whatever is left, you will frequently end up shortchanging it. So choose to pay for your savings first. This will help you effectively cut back on your expenses.

73 Get rid of cable TV.

A lot of people spend too much time in front of the television, a pastime that is not exactly productive. Instead of spending on cable subscription, you can choose to download or rent DVDs online and only watch the movies worth watching and not spend time scanning useless shows you find on TV most of the time.

74 Choose to use online savings instead of traditional bank savings accounts.

There are a number of online banks that offer twice as much interest than the normal banks. However, you will not get an ATM account or be provided with a convenient way to withdraw funds. This of course can work to your advantage since you can effectively curb the inclination to purchase things on impulse.

75 Choose to find happiness in life and not in spending.

A lot of people choose to buy stuff thinking subconsciously that it will help them find lasting happiness. These are the consumers who always feel the need to have the latest gadget, the fanciest car or the most popular pair of shoes. Truth is, when you buy stuff, you will be happy with your purchase for about a day or two at most.

After that, you will again feel the need to buy some more, which becomes a never---ending vicious cycle. Instead, choose to love and enjoy life. You can choose to find joy in nature and the people around you or perhaps in doing things that you really love. There are so many things in life that can provide you more happiness, all without the need to spend.

76 Turn your hobby into a profitable venture.

The thought of doing something you are extremely passionate about and making profit out of it is too good of an idea to pass up. If you love dabbling with web design, hone your craft and consider monetizing your creativity by taking on logo projects and web design projects on the side. If you love cycling, you can earn extra income by repairing and maintaining bikes. People who love to bake are making a small fortune selling their creations or some high---end cookware sets.

77 Learn to use your credit cards strategically.

Choose the right credit card to complement your spending habits so you can make the most of using credit cards. Choose cards that give reward points for purchasing things that you normally spend on. So before merely using a card because it's available, make an effort to study what card to best use to purchase what.

78 Consider engaging in paid testing.

Become a paid tester. There are a lot of medical companies as well as cosmetic developers that pay testers to personally try their treatments and products. In order to become eligible, you will need to meet a certain set of requirements.

79 Make blood plasma donation.

Unknown to many, blood plasma is a relatively high in demand commodity. The great thing about making blood plasma donation is the fact that you can actually go in and donate twice in 7 days, just as long as you have at least 2 days in between. You can generally get about $20 to $35 for every pint.

80 Discover earning money through recycling.

Try to check out if there are any recycling facilities near your locality. There are many towns that have several scrap metal recycling facilities, which can pay you for every pound of metal you bring in. In addition, if you live in a state where you are required to pay a deposit for every glass bottle, choose to return them to get the deposit, instead of throwing them out. However, keep in mind that it is illegal to do this across the state lines.

81 Take on some odd jobs.

If have the knowledge and expertise to do repairs, cleanups or yard work, you can make sure quick cash offering your services for such jobs. In fact, if you own a truck, you can offer your services to haul away debris and earn serious money when done on a regular basis.

82 Get a promotion.

If you are not really comfortable of the idea of asking for a salary raise, the next best thing you can do is earning that raise by getting a job promotion. It's a widely accepted fact that if you do more, you are expected to be paid more. So how about working towards advancing your career and earning that promotion? Of course, that would mean you need to perform well and take the necessary steps to highlight your achievements in a subtle way. However, you need to check if there is really room for growth in your company. If a promotion and a salary raise seem out of reach, you may want to set your sights elsewhere.

83 Sell handmade products on Etsy.

If you have a skill of coming up with creative things, you can put up an online store at Etsy and sell your products. A lot of consumers nowadays prefer customized and unique products – from handmade wedding invites to decorative pieces, check out a lot of inspiring DIY ideas you can cash on at Pinterest.com.

Money Stacking
84 Change your perception and attitude towards money.

As an employer, you are paid with money to render services. As an entrepreneur, you earn money by selling and delivering certain products and services. Money, contrary to how many people feel about it is not the root of all evils. However it is also not the panacea for all your pains along with the world's problems and ills. Money is simply an instrument ------ a tool that allows you to achieve a certain standard of living that you choose to pursue.

85 Change how you think about yourself.

You cannot define your character based on running balance or how much money you earn every month. However, you need to have the mindset that whatever amount you earn, you are worth it. If you believe you are a $30, 000 per year employee, shooting for $100, 000 is definitely quite a mind leap. Be ready to make the necessary career and life choices to enhance your personal ability to earn more money. Instead of "settling" for a job that simply brings food to the table, if you are confident you are worth more, you need to make the necessary steps to turn things around and take better control of your finances.

86 Choose to build your career based on income potential. The basic truth is we all work for money. And as you already know, there are some jobs than pay more, all without the need to put in extra hours of backbreaking work. If your primary motivation is earning more money, then make sure to choose a career where you can earn more. Set your goals and take the necessary steps to move up the career ladder.

87 Take time to check your credit score.

A lot of people don't know that one of the fastest ways to save a couple of thousand dollars is to check your credit score rating and fix error on your report. By taking time to improve your credit score, you can potentially save thousands on interest rates every year.

88 Make money by blogging.

If you have extra time on your hands, blogging is a great way to earn extra income. While this does not give you quick cash, with several months of solid and consistent effort, you can actually make a decent income. Get started by securing a nice domain name and get hosting service then set up your blog.

89 Write product reviews.

There are a number of online sites that pay you a small amount of cash by writing product reviews. If you write fast and knowledgeable, this may be a great side job for you.

90 Stage homes.

With the growing number of people selling houses and dealing with the all too real possibility of foreclosure, you can help people sell their homes by staging it for a quick sale. If you have a flair for design, then go ahead and offer your services.

91 Plan out your meals at least a week ahead and create your grocery list based on the menu plan.

Money Stacking

This will not only save you time, stress and money, it also makes it supremely easier to stick to healthier diets instead of succumbing to fast-food and processed products.

92 Step away from your computer.

The online world has open up a virtual place teeming with distractions. In order to increase your productivity, try to do most of your work offline.

93 If you are fond of watching TV, invest in Tivo.

Consider using DVR or Tivo to effectively cut down one hour television show down to 40 minutes.

94 Choose to auto--pay your bills.

Through making use of an automated system, you will save time processing payments and going to payment centers. In addition, you also eliminate those late fees as well as increased interest rates for missed payments.

95 Learn important keyboard shortcuts.

Knowing shortcuts will save you a considerable amount of time, so try to learn shorter keyboard commands, such as Ctrl +S to save, etc. This is especially useful if your work requires you to work on a computer on a regular basis.

96 Choose to get up earlier.

Going about your chores while everyone else is asleep and the house is still quiet will cut down work in a fraction of the time you usually spend. This is a very practical solution if you have small children running around, which makes it almost impossible to conduct a decent cleanup.

97 Choose to shop online whenever it's possible.

Instead of going through racks upon racks of clothing, shoes, or any other consumer items, by opting to shop online, you can cut down shopping time, gas expense, and curb impulse buying. This is especially helpful and a practical option during the holidays. If you don't exactly relish the thought of joining the rest of a few hundred other shoppers, then do your shopping online.

98 Invest in speeding up your Internet by getting broadband connection.

If your work and productivity greatly relies on your access to the internet, then it's only feasible that you ensure you have a stable, reliable connection.

99 Work on improving your typing speed.

Whether it's writing an email or an article or just about any other task that requires encoding, you can save a significant amount of time by increasing your typing speed.

100. Get Caller ID so you can avoid those unnecessary phone time.

Avoid calls that are not particularly important and prevent these from distracting you from you work.

As you may have found out from the tips provided, earning more and becoming successful doesn't have to be something exceptionally brilliant. You don't need to the inventor to the next best thing set to topple Facebook. You also don't have to be rocket scientist or a celebrity to build your own fortune.

Instead of focusing on large, ambitious goals, take time to go through the day to day activities you normally do and discover some innovative things to cut down time and save money. Again, success is the sum of all these small things.

Try to adapt practical habits and a minimalist lifestyle. You don't need all those trappings to flaunt your success or make you feel good about yourself. Choose to edit, delete and simplify your life. Seek rewarding things and do away with activities that only cause you to waste time and money needlessly.

You will realize that by making small changes on how you do things as well as your perspective on life and material stuff, you can actually cut down on unnecessary expenses and free up more of your time.

The solution to earning more is actually learning to spend less and pursuing your strengths. Consciously choose not to overcomplicated things and avoid unnecessary distractions that sidetrack you from your goals.

Once you have managed all these, you will find the rewards are truly promising.

ABOUT THE AUTHOR

Steve Mason is a well-known businessman and a business analyst in the country. Not only he wants to earn more money but he also wants to help others gain money and have financial stability. That is why he wrote this book to be an instrument to help others achieve financial growth.

Steve has a pretty wife Amanda and they live in Virginia.

www.ingramcontent.com/pod-product-compliance
Lightning Source LLC
Chambersburg PA
CBHW051241170526
45165CB00004B/1523